Contents

Introduction

If you are wild about learning and wild about animals – this book is for you!

It will take you on a wild adventure, where you will practise key addition and subtraction skills and explore the amazing world of animals along the way.

Each addition and subtraction topic is introduced in a clear and simple way with lots of interesting activities to complete so that you can practise what you have learned.

Alongside every addition and subtraction topic you will uncover fascinating facts about the animals who live in the Arctic and Antarctica.

When you have completed each topic, record the animals that you have seen and the skills that you have learned in the explorer's logbook on pages 28–29.

Good luck, explorer!

Alan Dobbs

Addition and number value

When you **add** positive numbers, the answer is always a number with a higher **value**.

Look at this addition: **2 + 2 = 4**

By adding together **2** and **2** you have a total of **4**

4 has a higher value than the two numbers that you started with.

4 has a higher value than **2** on the number line.

```
          1     2     3     4
    <----+-----+-----+-----+------->
Lower                          Higher
```

Task 1   Complete this number line.

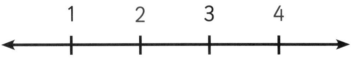

```
  [ ]   2   [ ] [ ]   5   [ ] [ ]   8   [ ] [ ]
  <--+---+---+---+---+---+---+---+---+---+---+-->
Lower                                    Higher
```

WILD FACT

Arctic terns fight to protect their chicks. They dive and attack anything that comes near them. They will even peck a polar bear!

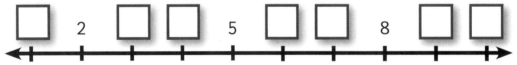

2

Task 2 Count the Arctic terns to answer these additions.

a 🐦🐦🐦 + 🐦🐦 = _____

b 🐦🐦🐦🐦🐦 + 🐦🐦🐦 _____

c 🐦🐦 + 🐦🐦🐦🐦 _____

d Which group of terns has the highest value: **a**, **b** or **c**? _____

Task 3 Answer these additions.

a 2 + 3 = _____   b 1 + 2 = _____

c 3 + 4 = _____   d 1 + 1 = _____

Write the totals from each sum in order of value, lowest to highest.

e _____ _____ _____ _____

Least value ⟶ Most value

WILD FACT

An Arctic tern may be small, but it is mighty! It makes a 70,000 km journey every year from Greenland in the far north to Antarctica in the far south.

Now glide over to pages 28–29 and fill in your explorer's logbook!

Subtracting

Subtracting (or difference between) means taking away. When we subtract positive numbers, the answer is always less than the numbers that we begin with.

Look at this subtraction: **4 − 1 = 3**

We begin with **4** and subtract (or take away) **1**. We have **3** left.

Task 1

Subtract these narwhals.

a _____ − _____ = _____

b _____ − _____ = _____

c _____ − _____ = _____

FACT FILE

Animal: Narwhal

I live in: Cold oceans around the Arctic and Greenland

I eat: Shrimps, fish and crabs

Task 2 Use the number line to help you answer these subtractions.

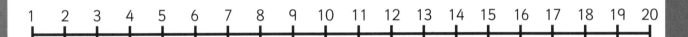

1 2 3 4 5 6 7 8 9 10 11 12 13 14 15 16 17 18 19 20

a Start at **9** and subtract **3** _____

b Start at **18** and subtract **6** _____

c Start at **15** and subtract **8** _____

d Start at **17** and subtract **5** _____

Task 3 Answer these subtractions. Use the number line in Task 2 to help you.

a 12 – 4 = _____

b 20 – 6 = _____

c 17 – 9 = _____

d 16 – 3 = _____

Now swim over to pages 28–29 and fill in your explorer's logbook!

Adding 3 numbers

We can add more than 2 numbers.

Here, 3 numbers have been added: **3 + 2 + 1 = 6**

We add all the numbers to find the total.

FACT FILE

Animal: Krill
I live in: All the world's oceans
I eat: Tiny sea plants

| Task 1 | Add the krill to find the totals. |

a [krill] + [krill] + [krill] = _____

b [krill] + [krill] + [krill] = _____

c [krill] + [krill] + [krill] = _____

Task 2   Write the answers to these additions.

a 2 + 4 + 1 = _____

b 5 + 3 + 2 = _____

c 6 + 2 + 4 = _____

d 1 + 7 + 2 = _____

Task 3   Answer these additions.

a **3 + 2 + 4** =   _____

b **7 + 4 + 2** =   _____

c **10 + 4 + 6** =   _____

d **2 + 6 + 3** =   _____

WILD FACT

Krill may be tiny, but they are eaten by the world's largest sea creature – the whale.

Now swim over to pages 28–29 and fill in your explorer's logbook!

Order and addition

FACT FILE
Animal: Greenland shark
I live in: Deep cold water
I eat: Fish and rotting animals

We can do addition in any order. This is known as **commutative**.

Look at these additions:

3 + 2 + 1 = 6   2 + 1 + 3 = 6   1 + 2 + 3 = 6

Whatever order we write the numbers in the addition, the total is always the same.

WILD FACT

The Greenland shark is one of the largest sharks in the world. It is almost as long as the great white shark!

Task 1   Write the answers to these additions. Then write the additions in a different order. An example has been done for you.

2 + 4 = ___6___   ___4___ + ___2___ = ___6___

a 6 + 4 = _____   _____ + _____ = _____

b 12 + 3 = _____   _____ + _____ = _____

c 15 + 6 = _____   _____ + _____ = _____

Task 2

Answer these additions and then write the addition twice more with the numbers in a different order each time. An example has been done for you.

$12 + 4 + 5 = \underline{\;21\;}$

$\underline{\;5\;} + \underline{\;4\;} + \underline{\;12\;} = \underline{\;21\;}$

$\underline{\;4\;} + \underline{\;12\;} + \underline{\;5\;} = \underline{\;21\;}$

a $13 + 2 + 4 = \underline{\qquad}$

$\underline{\qquad} + \underline{\qquad} + \underline{\qquad} = \underline{\qquad}$

$\underline{\qquad} + \underline{\qquad} + \underline{\qquad} = \underline{\qquad}$

b $16 + 3 + 1 = \underline{\qquad}$

$\underline{\qquad} + \underline{\qquad} + \underline{\qquad} = \underline{\qquad}$

$\underline{\qquad} + \underline{\qquad} + \underline{\qquad} = \underline{\qquad}$

c $10 + 6 + 4 = \underline{\qquad}$

$\underline{\qquad} + \underline{\qquad} + \underline{\qquad} = \underline{\qquad}$

$\underline{\qquad} + \underline{\qquad} + \underline{\qquad} = \underline{\qquad}$

WILD FACT

Many Greenland sharks have small sea creatures dangling from their eyes. These creatures damage the sharks' eyes and can make them blind.

Task 3

Write two additions for each set of 3 numbers. Then write the answers.

| 6 | 8 | 2 |

a $\underline{\qquad} + \underline{\qquad} = \underline{\qquad}$ $\underline{\qquad} + \underline{\qquad} = \underline{\qquad}$

| 5 | 9 | 4 |

b $\underline{\qquad} + \underline{\qquad} = \underline{\qquad}$ $\underline{\qquad} + \underline{\qquad} = \underline{\qquad}$

Now glide slowly over to pages 28–29 and fill in your explorer's logbook!

Order and subtraction

Unlike addition, subtraction cannot be done in any order and still have the same answer.

Here are 3 Arctic foxes.

We cannot take 4 foxes away from these 3, as there are not enough foxes!

Task 1   Write these subtractions as numbers and find the answers.

   =

a _____ – _____ = _____

b _____ – _____ = _____

c _____ – _____ = _____

Task 2

Join the subtractions to the correct answers. One has been done for you.

10 − 3 = ——→ 9

20 − 5 = ——→ 7

12 − 7 =   15

14 − 5 =   5

Task 3

Write the missing number to make these subtractions correct.

a 6 − _____ = 3

b _____ − 4 = 6

c 12 − _____ = 11

d _____ − 10 = 10

Now trot over to pages 28–29 and fill in your explorer's logbook!

Additions and subtractions

Addition and subtraction can be mixed.

Look at this mixed addition and subtraction:

$$3 + 4 - 2 = 5$$

Add the first two numbers: $3 + 4 = 7$

Then subtract the final number: $7 - 2$

This gives the answer: $= 5$

FACT FILE

Animal: Southern elephant seal
I live in: Water and ice around Antarctica
I eat: Fish, crabs and octopus

Task 1 Work out the answers to these calculations.

a 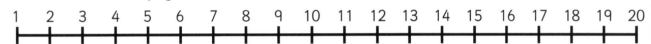 🦀🦀🦀🦀 + 🦀🦀🦀 – 🦀 = _____

b 🦀🦀 + 🦀🦀🦀 – 🦀🦀 = _____

c 🦀🦀🦀🦀🦀 + 🦀🦀 – 🦀🦀🦀 = _____

Task 2 Answer these calculations. Use the number line to help you.

```
1   2   3   4   5   6   7   8   9   10  11  12  13  14  15  16  17  18  19  20
├───┼───┼───┼───┼───┼───┼───┼───┼───┼───┼───┼───┼───┼───┼───┼───┼───┼───┼───┤
```

a 12 + 3 – 5 = _____

b 10 + 6 – 4 = _____

c 15 + 4 – 6 = _____

d 17 + 2 – 3 = _____

WILD FACT

Elephant seals are named after their large snouts, which look quite like an elephant's trunk!

Task 3 Answer these calculations. Be careful to check what each sum is asking!

a 15 – 3 + 6 = _____

b 12 – 8 + 7 = _____

c 13 – 5 + 3 = _____

Now dive over to pages 28–29 and fill in your explorer's logbook!

Quantities

When an amount of something is counted, it is known as a **quantity**. We can add and subtract quantities, just like numbers.

Task 1   This is the quantity of clams that a sea otter eats each day.

a How many clams would 2 sea otters eat in 1 day? _____

b Write the calculation that shows this. _____

c What quantity of clams would 3 otters eat in 1 day?

_____

d Write the calculation that shows this. _____

WILD FACT

Sea otters spend much of their time floating. They can break the shells of clams and crabs using a stone. They float upside down and rest their food on their bellies!

Task 2 Here are some different quantities of clams and crabs.

a How many clams are there? _____

b How many crabs are there? _____

c What is the total quantity of clams and crabs together? _____

d Write this as an addition. _____

WILD FACT

Sea otters spend a lot of time sleeping. To stop themselves drifting away, they tie themselves to seaweed!

Task 3 Look at the quantity of sea creatures in this picture.

a How many creatures are there altogether? _____

b Subtract 4 creatures from the total. _____

c Write this as a subtraction. _____

Now float over to pages 28–29 and fill in your explorer's logbook!

Measurements

When we add or subtract **measurements**, we must make sure that the unit of measurement is included in the answer.

Here is an example:

We measure length in metres and centimetres. These two walruses measure different lengths. Walrus **A** measures 3 metres (m) and walrus **B** measures 2 m. Together, their total length equals 5 m.

A | 1 metre | 1 metre | 1 metre |

B | 1 metre | 1 metre |

3 m + 2 m = 5 m

Task 1 Walrus **A** is 2 metres (m) tall. Walrus **B** is 1 m tall. Answer these questions. Remember to include the units in your answer.

A

2 metres tall

B

1 metre tall

a How much taller is walrus **A** than walrus **B**? _____

b Write this as a subtraction. _____

c What are the heights of walrus **A** and walrus **B** added together?

_____

d Write this as an addition. _____

Task 2 We measure capacity in litres (l). We can add litres just like we add other quantities. Remember to write the unit **l**, for litres!

Each bottle contains 1 litre (l) of milk.

a Pup **X** drank: 🍾 + 🍾 + 🍾 + 🍾 _____

b Pup **Y** drank 3 more litres of milk than pup **X**.

How many litres did pup **Y** drink? _____

c Pup **Z** drank 1 litre less than pup **X**. How many

litres did pup **Z** drink? _____

Before diving into the freezing water, walruses like to sunbathe. They turn bright pink as the sun warms them!

Task 3 We measure mass in kilograms and grams. Look at this problem.

12 kg + 7 kg – 6 kg

a Answer the calculation. _____

b Add 3 kg to your answer. _____

c Subtract 2 kg from this new total. _____

Now dive over to pages 28–29 and fill in your explorer's logbook!

Understanding inverse

We know that we can add in any order.

1 + 2 + 3 = 6   and   **2 + 3 + 1 = 6**

Inverse means opposite. Subtraction is the **opposite**, or inverse, of addition.

We can check an addition or a subtraction using the inverse.

2 + 3 = 5   and   **5 – 3 = 2**

Task 1 Write the inverse of each calculation. An example has been done for you.

3 + 4 = 7   7 – 4 = 3

a 6 + 4 = 10 _____

b 12 – 5 = 7 _____

c 15 + 5 = 20 _____

WILD FACT

Emperor penguins like to 'sledge' on the ice. They slide along, pushing themselves with their feet!

Task 2 Write **+** or **−** to make these calculations correct.

a 13 ___ 5 = 18   18 ___ 5 = 13

b 20 ___ 7 = 13   13 ___ 7 = 20

c 17 ___ 2 = 19   19 ___ 2 = 17

Task 3 Answer these questions.

a Write a 2-number addition that equals 20. _____

b What is the inverse of this?   _____

c Write a subtraction that equals 20.   _____

d What is the inverse of this?   _____

Now sledge over to pages 28–29 and fill in your explorer's logbook!

19

Fact families

If we know that **7 + 3 = 10**

we know all the additions and subtractions for these numbers:

3 + 7 = 10   **10 – 7 = 3**   **10 – 3 = 7**

This is called a **fact family**.

We can also make fact families with 2-digit numbers.

If you know that **10 + 20 = 30**

then **20 + 10 = 30** and **30 – 10 = 20** and **30 – 20 = 10**

Task 1

Write the fact family for each set of numbers. An example has been done for you.

1 2 3   **1 + 2 = 3**   **2 + 1 = 3**   **3 − 1 = 2**   **3 − 2 = 1**

a 4 5 9   _____   _____   _____   _____

b 10 5 15   _____   _____   _____   _____

c 14 5 19   _____   _____   _____   _____

Task 2

Write the fact families for these 2-digit numbers.

a 30 50 80   _____   _____   _____   _____

b 20 40 60   _____   _____   _____   _____

c 20 70 90   _____   _____   _____   _____

WILD FACT

Polar bears have black skin, which helps them to soak up the sun and keep warm.

Task 3

Write fact families for the number 100 using 2 2-digit numbers from the boxes below. An example has been done for you using 80 and 20.

[30]   [40]   [60]   [70]   [10]   [90]

80 + 20 = 100   20 + 80 = 100   100 − 80 = 20   100 − 20 = 80

a _____   _____   _____   _____

b _____   _____   _____   _____

c _____   _____   _____   _____

Now swim over to pages 28–29 and fill in your explorer's logbook!

21

2-digit numbers

When adding or subtracting 2-digit numbers, the **ones** need to be added or subtracted first and then the **tens**.

Here is an example of addition. The ones are shown in red and the tens in blue.

25 + 12 = 37

Follow these steps:

Ones:	Tens:	Totals:
5 + 2 = 7	20 + 10 = 30	30 + 7 = 37

Here is an example of subtraction:

28 – 15 = 13

Follow these steps:

Ones:	Tens:	Totals:
8 – 5 = 3	20 – 10 = 10	10 + 3 = 13

Using columns helps with adding and subtracting. You must still add or subtract the ones before the tens.

23 + 14 would look like this:

Tens	Ones
2	3
1	4 +
3	7

23 + 14 = 37

Task 1 Use a separate sheet to work out these additions and subtractions. Write your answers below.

a 21 + 24 = _____

b 36 + 42 = _____

c 29 – 16 = _____

d 47 – 16 = _____

Task 2

Add or subtract the ones and then the tens. Then write the answers.

	Ones	Tens	
a 13 + 15	_____	_____	**13 + 15 = _____**
b 32 – 12	_____	_____	**32 – 12 = _____**
c 45 + 23	_____	_____	**45 + 23 = _____**

Task 3

These additions are in columns.
Add the ones, then the tens.

a Tens	Ones	b Tens	Ones	c Tens	Ones
3	5	4	1	2	3
+2	4	+3	6	+1	5
_____		_____		_____	
_____		_____		_____	

WILD FACT

Woolly bear caterpillars can stay alive even when they are frozen solid!

Now munch your way over to pages 28–29 and fill in your explorer's logbook!

Problem solving

We can use addition or subtraction to solve maths problems. Use your skills to answer the following questions.

FACT FILE

Animal: Orca (killer whale)
I live in: Cold waters around the Arctic and Antarctic
I eat: Fish and other sea creatures

WILD FACT

Orcas live in family groups called pods. There can be up to 60 orcas in a single pod!

Task 1   Answer these word problems.

a An orca ate 5 fish in the morning and 7 fish at lunchtime. How many fish did the orca eat in total? _____

b Show the addition you used to work out the answer.

_____

c A pod has 16 orcas. 3 orcas leave the pod. How many orcas are left? _____

d Show the subtraction you used.

_____

Task 2   Now try these word problems.

a An orca swims 10 kilometres (km) to find food. It swims another 3 km while playing. Finally, the orca swims 4 km to find its pod. How far does the orca swim in total?

_____ km

b Show the addition for this problem.

_____

c A pod of orcas meets with a second pod. The first pod has 23 orcas. The second pod has 6 orcas fewer. How many orcas are in the second pod?

_____

d Show the subtraction for this problem.

_____

Task 3   Now try these number problems.

a 12 calves (baby orcas) are born in a pod of 32 orcas. How many orcas are there in the pod now?

_____

b Show the calculation. _____

c A male orca measures 9 metres (m) and a female is 2 m shorter. What is the length of the female orca?

_____ m

d Show the calculation. _____

Now splash over to pages 28–29 and fill in your explorer's logbook!

Quick test

Now try these questions. Give yourself 1 mark for every correct answer.

1 **Complete this number line.**

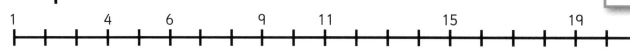

2 **Answer these calculations.**

a 6 + 5 – 3 = _____

b 10 + 7 – 5 = _____

c 16 + 3 – 2 = _____

3 **Write the missing addition (+) and subtraction (–) signs.**

a 15 ___ 5 = 10

b 20 ___ 6 = 26

c 13 ___ 3 ___ 5 = 11

4 **Write these additions in a different order.**

a 2 + 3 + 7 = 12   _____ + _____ + _____ = 12

b 10 + 1 + 9 = 20   _____ + _____ + _____ = 20

c 1 + 7 + 6 = 14   _____ + _____ + _____ = 14

5 **Write the numbers that make these additions and subtractions correct.**

a 15 + _____ = 20

b 16 – _____ = 9

c _____ + 6 = 10

6 **Write the fact family for these numbers: 12   5   17**

_____   _____

_____   _____

7 Add or subtract the lengths.

   a 13 cm + 4 cm + 2 cm = _____ cm

   b 10 m – 6 m = _____ m

   c 20 cm – 10 cm = _____ cm

   d 2 km + 10 km – 3 km = _____ km

8 Write this as a number calculation.

_____ = _____

9 10 woolly bear caterpillars meet 6 others. How many woolly bear caterpillars are there now?

_____

10 Answer these column additions.

a Tens	Ones		b Tens	Ones		c Tens	Ones
5	5		6	7		7	3
+2	4		+2	2		+1	5
___	___		___	___		___	___
___	___		___	___		___	___

11 Show the steps to solve this subtraction.

25 – 12 _____ _____ _____ 25 – 12 = _____

12 Solve these problems.

   a 2 Arctic terns have 5 chicks each. How many chicks are there in total?

   _____

   b Show this as an addition.

   _____

How did you do? 1–5 Try again! 6–10 Good try!
11–15 Great work! 16–26 Excellent exploring!

/26

Explorer's Logbook

Tick off the topics as you complete them and then colour in the star.

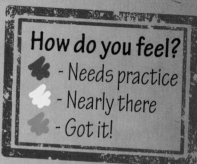

Addition and number value ☐

Subtracting ☐

Adding 3 numbers ☐

Order and addition ☐

Order and subtraction ☐

Additions and subtractions ☐

Quantities ☐

Measurements ☐

Understanding inverse ☐

Fact families ☐

2-digit numbers ☐

Problem solving ☐

Answers

Pages 2–3
Task 1

Lower   Higher

Task 2

a 5   **b** 8   **c** 6   **d** b

Task 3

a 5   **b** 3   **c** 7   **d** 2

e 2, 3, 5, 7 (d, b, a, c)

Pages 4–5
Task 1

a 3   **b** 3   **c** 1

Task 2

a 6   **b** 12   **c** 7   **d** 12

Task 3

a 8   **b** 14   **c** 8   **d** 13

Pages 6–7
Task 1

a 7   **b** 8   **c** 11

Task 2

a 7   **b** 10   **c** 12   **d** 10

Task 3

a 9   **b** 13   **c** 20   **d** 11

Pages 8–9
Task 1

a $6 + 4 = 10$ $4 + 6 = 10$

b $12 + 3 = 15$ $3 + 12 = 15$

c $15 + 6 = 21$ $6 + 15 = 21$

Task 2

a $13 + 2 + 4 = 19$; any other combinations of numbers being added

b $16 + 3 + 1 = 20$; any other combinations of numbers being added

c $10 + 6 + 4 = 20$; any other combinations of numbers being added

Task 3

a $6 + 2 = 8$ $2 + 6 = 8$

b $5 + 4 = 9$ $4 + 5 = 9$

Pages 10–11
Task 1

a $3 - 2 = 1$ **b** $5 - 3 = 2$ **c** $6 - 2 = 4$

Task 2

$10 - 3 = 7$ $20 - 5 = 15$ $12 - 7 = 5$ $14 - 5 = 9$

Task 3

a $6 - 3 = 3$ **b** $10 - 4 = 6$

c $12 - 1 = 11$ **d** $20 - 10 = 10$

Pages 12–13
Task 1

a $4 + 3 - 1 = 6$ **b** $2 + 3 - 2 = 3$ **c** $5 + 2 - 3 = 4$

Task 2

a 10   **b** 12   **c** 13   **d** 16

Task 3

a 18   **b** 11   **c** 11

Pages 14–15
Task 1

a 16   **b** $8 + 8 = 16$

c 24   **d** $8 + 8 + 8 = 24$

Task 2

a 11   **b** 11   **c** 22   **d** $11 + 11 = 22$

Task 3

a 9   **b** 5   **c** $9 - 4 = 5$

Pages 16–17
Task 1

a 1 m   **b** $2m - 1m = 1m$

c 3 m   **d** $2m + 1m = 3m$

Task 2

a 4 l   **b** 7 l   **c** 3 l

Task 3

a $12 kg + 7 kg - 6 kg = 13 kg$

b $13 kg + 3 kg = 16 kg$

c $16 kg - 2 kg = 14 kg$

Pages 18–19
Task 1

a $10 - 4 = 6$ or $10 - 6 = 4$

b $7 + 5 = 12$ or $5 + 7 = 12$

c $20 - 5 = 15$ or $20 - 15 = 5$

Task 2

a $13 + 5 = 18$ $18 - 5 = 13$

b $20 - 7 = 13$ $13 + 7 = 20$

c $17 + 2 = 19$ $19 - 2 = 17$

Task 3

a Any two numbers that equal 20, for example, $18 + 2 = 20$

b A subtraction, for example, $20 - 2 = 18$

c Any two numbers that equal 20, for example, $25 - 5 = 20$

d An addition, for example, $20 + 5 = 25$

Pages 20 – 21
Task 1

a $4 + 5 = 9$ $5 + 4 = 9$ $9 - 4 = 5$ $9 - 5 = 4$

b $10 + 5 = 15$ $5 + 10 = 15$ $15 - 10 = 5$ $15 - 5 = 10$

c $14 + 5 = 19$ $5 + 14 = 19$ $19 - 14 = 5$ $19 - 5 = 14$

Task 2

a 30 + 50 = 80   50 + 30 = 80
   80 − 30 = 50   80 − 50 = 30
b 20 + 40 = 60   40 + 20 = 60
   60 − 20 = 40   60 − 40 = 20
c 20 + 70 = 90   70 + 20 = 90
   90 − 20 = 70   90 − 70 = 20

Task 3

a 30 + 70 = 100   70 + 30 = 100
   100 − 30 = 70   100 − 70 = 30
b 40 + 60 = 100   60 + 40 = 100
   100 − 40 = 60   100 − 60 = 40
c 10 + 90 = 100   90 + 10 = 100
   100 − 10 = 90   100 − 90 = 10

Pages 22–23

Task 1

a 45   **b** 78   **c** 13   **d** 31

Task 2

a 3 + 5 = 8   10 + 10 = 20   13 + 15 = 28
b 2 − 2 = 0   30 − 10 = 20   32 − 12 = 20
c 5 + 3 = 8   40 + 20 = 60   45 + 23 = 68

Task 3

a 59   **b** 77   **c** 38

Pages 24–25

Task 1

a 12   **b** 5 + 7 = 12
c 13   **d** 16 − 3 = 13

Task 2

a 17 km   **b** 10 km + 3 km + 4 km = 17 km
c 17   **d** 23 − 6 = 17

Task 3

a 44 orcas   **b** 32 + 12 = 44
c 7 m   **d** 9 m − 2 m = 7 m

Pages 26–27

1 1 2 3 4 5 6 7 8 9 10 11 12 13 14 15 16 17 18 19 20

2 a 8   **b** 12   **c** 17
3 a 15 − 5 = 10   **b** 20 + 6 = 26
   c 13 + 3 − 5 = 11
4 Any different combination of the numbers being added
5 a 15 + 5 = 20   **b** 16 − 7 = 9
   c 4 + 6 = 10
6 12 + 5 = 17   5 + 12 = 17   17 − 12 = 5   17 − 5 = 12
7 a 19 cm   **b** 4 m   **c** 10 cm   **d** 9 km
8 5 + 3 − 2 = 6
9 16
10 a 79   **b** 89   **c** 88
11 5 − 2 = 3   20 − 10 = 10   10 + 3 = 13   25 − 12 = 13
12 a 10
   b 5 + 5 = 10

Well done, explorer!

You have finished your addition and subtraction adventure!

Explorer's pass

Name: _____

Age: _____

Date: _____

Draw a picture of yourself in the box!